From Praying Never
To Praying Always

From Praying Never To Praying Always

MARY AMLAW

PUEBLO PUBLISHING COMPANY
New York

Design: Br. Aelred-Seton Shanley

Scriptural pericopes are from the New American Bible, copyright © 1970 by the Confraternity of Christian Doctrine, Washington, D.C. All rights reserved.

Copyright © 1985 Pueblo Publishing Company, Inc. 1860 Broadway, New York, N.Y. All rights reserved.

ISBN: 0-916134-69-5

Printed in the United States of America.

CONTENTS

ONE

Prayer: Calling on the God of Love

Do you find prayer boring? Is it something you force yourself to do, like taking prescribed medicine, because you are afraid of the consequences of not doing it?

We know prayer is not a priority when we go to the first Saturday afternoon Mass to "get it over with." Or when we wait until the last Mass on Sunday afternoon so our obligation to attend the liturgy won't spoil the weekend. And that is what prayer is, not a joyful refreshment, but a duty to be endured.

We would like to be more enthusiastic about prayer. Sometimes we sigh over our poor attitude; maybe we discuss it with a priest, hoping his response might make prayer more attractive. It doesn't. The next Sunday, even as we rise to hear the gospel, mentally we're out on the beach.

Weekday prayer fares worse. Most of us try to pray; some as a result of our upbringing, others from a sense of obligation or perhaps from a fear that God will see us as goats rather than sheep when he separates the flock on the final day. Our prayer may range from an occasional "God help me!" when things pile up, to a well-established routine that includes a morning offering, the Angelus, acts of faith, hope, charity, and contrition, novenas, even the rosary. Yet despite our best intentions, we find ourselves forcing our way through prayer, trying to stifle inner doubts that question whether it is worth doing. We don't enjoy prayer, we suffer it.

PRAY ALWAYS?

We know prayer is supposed to be central to the life of the soul. "Pray always," Jesus told us (Luke 21:36) without making it plain how to do so while dealing with small children, a challenging job, difficult in-laws, tax returns, and a myriad of daily worries.

Scripture shows us that Jesus prayed in all circumstances and at all times. In the morning, long before dawn, he got up and went off to a lonely place to pray (Mark 1:35). After the miracle of the loaves, he went into the hills to pray (Mark 6:47). Luke tells us that he would often go off to a place where he could be alone and pray (Luke 5:16). Before choosing the apostles from among his disciples, he spent the whole night in prayer (Luke 6:13). The gospel of John gives us prayer after prayer of Christ praising his Father and beseeching him on behalf of his followers.

It would be nice to tell ourselves Christ had so much time for prayer because he wasn't as busy as we are, but he was constantly besieged by people seeking cures, by Pharisees trying to discredit him, and by followers attracted to his teaching.

When Christ visited the home of the two sisters, Martha and Mary, Martha bustled about serving him and making him comfortable, while Mary sat quietly absorbing his teaching (Luke 10:38–41). We are convinced we too must be Marthas if our families are to eat regularly. Our lives don't allow us the luxury of sitting quietly at the feet of Christ, like Mary. Yet Christ told Martha, who fretted about being left with all the tasks of serving, that Mary had chosen the better portion (Luke 10:41).

Perhaps when we reach the brink of eternity and are free at last of earthly obligations prayer will hold an attraction for us. Meanwhile we struggle not to be submerged in the busyness of everyday life. As for serious prayer, we trust priests, religious, and holy souls who have given their lives to God to pray sufficiently to cover our lack.

We wonder at the saints, so drawn to prayer. Many, like St. Dominic, spent all night in prayer after a day of preaching and working for God. Others, like the child visionary Francisco of Fatima, found themselves drawn to the tabernacle for hours on end. Saints John Vianney, Joan of Arc, and Therese of Lisieux, and Blessed Anna Catherine Emmerich delighted in prayer even as children.

In our hearts, we are convinced such love of prayer is simply one more characteristic distinguishing the saints from us ordinary folk. God touched them in some mysterious way, and as a result, prayer attracted them like iron filings to a magnet. Maybe if we were having visions and working miracles, as they did, we would pray constantly, too. But we aren't saints. We are just everyday people leading everyday lives. We go to Mass, we make our Easter duty, we do as much good as we can. Is it our fault we find prayer a numbing, mindless, monotonous chore? If Christ truly meant us to "Pray always," surely he had something more in mind than this!

If boredom and monotony are all you have
experienced at prayer, then you have not
yet experienced prayer. "Saying prayers,"
no matter how many years you have given
to that practice, is not praying. We tend to
"say prayers" into a void, ritualistically
completing every word while our minds are
distracted, mulling over our affairs and
urging us to hurry up and finish so we can
get on with more pressing matters.

The catechism teaches that prayer is the
lifting of the heart and mind to God. If
there is no contact with God, there is no
prayer. We can mumble pious words night
and day, but as St. Teresa of Jesus of Avila,
the great Spanish mystic of the sixteenth
century, tells us in the first chapter of
Interior Castle: "If a person does not think
Whom he is addressing, and what he is
asking for, and who it is that is asking and
of Whom he is asking it, I do not consider
that he is praying at all even though he be
constantly moving his lips."

"Saying prayers," where only the mouth is
engaged while mind and heart are
uninvolved, is as far removed from praying
as a child's first grappling with "Für Elise"
is from a Horowitz piano recital. Since
there is nothing nourishing or attractive
found in it, our good common sense finds

the procedure stale and dull and resents wasting time on it.

What keeps us from lifting heart and mind to God? A clue surfaces in the recommendation of spiritual masters such as St. Ignatius of Loyola that the soul should begin prayer by calling itself into the presence of God. This means to recollect ourselves, to know we are standing before the Creator of all that is, the God who made us and to whom we must one day render an account of our lives.

Call ourselves into his stupendous presence? The very thought is enough to make us shudder. We prefer God to remain remote, thank you, the all-powerful Creator living in heaven, where his will is done. We would just as soon escape his notice, since we are sure, in our inmost hearts, that we don't measure up to his expectations. Even though Christ taught us that God is our loving Father, a deeper image persists of God as judge. To deliberately call ourselves into his presence seems foolhardy in the extreme. Death will call us into his presence soon enough. For most of us, the idea of coming to that final face-to-face meeting with God is the prime terror of death. We anticipate an experience similar to facing a tough teacher who tells us, rather gleefully, that we have failed the exam.

GOD AS JUDGE

God has a bad press. We blame him for every disaster. We attribute every illness, every hardship, every painful circumstance to him. At best we say he is purifying us, like gold in the furnace. At worst we say disaster proves God doesn't exist. For if we were God, with all power over all things, we would end all natural catastrophes, disarm the world, heal all the sick, feed the hungry, help people love one another. That is what *we* would do, if we had the power, and we certainly aren't all-good. God has the power to do anything. He has told us through Jesus that he is love, our loving Father. And we, blinded by the evils we see around us, challenge him: prove it, God!

Because we cannot see his goodness and love in terms we understand, we remain unconvinced of God's love. We pray at best with a divided heart, fearing lest our prayer attract the attention of a God who judges and purifies. We have enough difficulties without drawing down more! So we pray without praying, reciting words without thought; for when we let ourselves think about God, he frightens us. Surely he cannot be pleased with us, for we know only too well how ungodlike we are in our behavior. Yet we haven't the inclination to spend our lives actively trying to please him. He seems to be pleased by such unpleasant things!

Take the saints, for example. They please God—by penance, by mortification, by great hardship, often by martyrdom. What kind of God is pleased by this—and then says he is love? We decide if this is the way of God, then we'll stay with the way of the world. The world doesn't offer us eternal life, but it does entice us with real pleasures that help us endure times of pain.

The terror of meeting God lies in the question we dare not put into words. It is easier to veer away hastily from any thought of God at all, but the question persists. *What if God isn't love?* What if he is only justice, the judge with the power to sentence us forever? If we don't come too close, if we don't test him too severely, if we don't truly seek him in prayer, then we can cling to the idea that he *may* be love. Better to cling to that hope, the only barrier we have against the terror of death, than to approach God closely enough to remove all doubt.

God created the human race in a state of happiness where all our wants were supplied. We broke from God, not God from us. Yet we think of God banishing Adam and Eve from Eden, taking back the gifts he had given them, and condemning them and all their posterity to earning their bread by the sweat of their brow (Genesis 3:19), as if relishing the suffering the human race would undergo for disobeying him. We make God the bad guy.

Let's update the scenario. Your sixteen-year-old son complains that home is a prison and you the jailer. He is leaving to find freedom in the streets. You warn him that he is throwing away his future and his education; turning his back on your love; inviting danger, even death. Yet he prefers that to living with house rules you think eminently reasonable; no drugs, no drinking, no unchaperoned parties.

He leaves. He runs away. Can his mother cook for him now or see to it he gets nourishing meals? Can his father supervise his activities? He has broken the bond with you.

We turned away from our Father; we left home for the streets. And we complain when we find life as full of suffering as he warned us it would be. We fell away from love to no-love. In our misery, we blame God for letting us turn from him.

Why did he allow us to fall, knowing the hateful things we would face? For the same reason you don't chain your rebellious teenager in your house to keep him safe. If people are to love, they must have equal freedom to hate. If their coming together is to have meaning, they must also be free to go.

God did not intend us to be slaves, forced to bow to his will. He created us in freedom. Would you want a robot programmed to say "I love you, I love you, I love you," in preference to a live person whose love for you was a free gift? Neither does God.

Because he loves us too much to let us sink in our own folly, however, God sent his Son to show us the way home. Christ taught us of the loving concern God has for us: "The Father already loves you, because you have loved me and have believed that I came from God" (John 16:27). In the first letter of John we read: "God is love, and he who abides in love, abides in God, and God in him." (1 John 4:16). But these assurances remain only words until we experience God on a more immediate and personal level.

Have you ever been so in love you were willing to turn yourself inside out for your beloved, only to be ignored? Have you seen your beloved turn from you and choose another who was less loving, less sincere? Perhaps you tried to prove how great your love was, to no avail.

God is our rejected lover. He stands at the fringe of our lives, the very life he has given us, and watches us turn away from him. We put our fingers in our ears to shut out his plaintive voice, close our eyes to blind ourselves to his presence, and busy ourselves with everyone and everything but him.

God is love. All that we have of love comes ultimately from him. We love in spurts and starts, our love laced with self-seeking, with anger, with indifference, our affection waxing and waning. God loves constantly. His love is never more or less, never withdrawn or tainted with self-interest. It is pure and infinite, so all-encompassing that with it we can endure anything, while without it there is lasting pleasure in nothing. His love completes and sustains us. It transforms us, and in transforming us illuminates our lives.

OBSTACLES TO LOVING

The saints were aware constantly of God's love. More than one saint, enduring severe physical suffering, has reported to onlookers that although all could see and shrink from their suffering, only they could see the joy, and the joy was far greater. We think skeptically that saints are supposed to say such things. Saints are strange creatures who love to call themselves worms and to revel in suffering. Psychologists have a word for them—masochists.

Saints, we tell ourselves, were so continually reassured by visions and revelations that their sufferings made little impression on them. They sailed through the rougher passages of life with aplomb, scarcely more affected by suffering and hardship than an actor playing a harrowing role in a play. They lived with one foot in heaven and their earthly trials rolled over them without leaving a mark.

Our troubles can't be dismissed so easily. We live in a world of economic crisis, injustice, and saber-rattling, nuclear-armed nations. We endure everything from inefficient subway systems to the bombardment of drugs and pornography that rains down on our children. We suffer the agony of watching our loved ones succumb to illness and death. We can't help asking ourselves, if God is so loving, why doesn't he show it? Why doesn't he stop these evils, or at least ameliorate them for us? Doesn't he care enough to help us? Isn't he able to?

In the *Dialogue* of St. Catherine of Siena, God replies to these and similar questions that have long troubled human beings. "Tribulations on man's account, or infirmity, or poverty, or change of worldly condition, or loss of children or of other much loved creatures," he tells her, "are thorns that the earth produced after sin." He reminds her that he is the Supreme Good, "Who cannot desire other than good, for which I permit these tribulations through love and not through hatred." He explains how these things profit souls and enrich them in virtues, and he reminds her again and again of his love, which he proved by dying for us.

When humanity turned from God, we destroyed the bridge from heaven to earth, an act of destruction beyond our ability to repair. In turning away from God, we gave the deed of earth into the hands of Satan, in effect telling God his intervention in our affairs was not wanted. The prince of this world, Christ calls Satan in scripture, adding that, "He has no hold on me" (John 14:30). Christ has delivered us from evil. He became the bridge from earth to heaven, ". . . and cemented [the stones] with His blood."

If your rebellious teenager, after leaving home, involves himself with criminals, can you extricate him against his will? Even if you had the resources to do so, what would be the point? He would only return to them, in spite of your love for him and your attempts to free him.

But if your son reaches out to you, admits he has made a mistake, and yearns to be restored to you, wouldn't you move heaven and earth to help him?

COME TO ME

"Come to me," Christ urged us (John 7:37), and he waits patiently for us to respond to his invitation. He presents us with opportunities to turn to him. He doesn't care if we respond out of a desire to love him, to do his will, or simply from a feeling of disillusionment and a hope that there must be more to life than we have found without him. By rights he should be insulted, but God loves us so foolishly he overlooks much in us, who in our ignorance hardly know more of him than his name.

The recommendation of St. Ignatius that we call ourselves into the presence of God is in a sense superfluous. We are always in his presence. When we call on him, we are picking up the receiver of a telephone where the caller has been on hold. We are not so much establishing contact as acknowledging it.

"God," we cry, "if you are there, please find me, because I can't find you."

Our call reaches God like the voice of your lost toddler, sobbing one aisle over in the supermarket. None of the goodies stacked on shelf after shelf entices your child if she has lost sight of you. She cries, and you respond. We cry, and God responds. He rushes to enfold us in himself, to envelop us in love.

We can't begin to comprehend the love God has for us. He burns with love, infinite love for each of us. His love encompasses every love. He loves us foolishly, like a lover besotted; he loves us tenderly, like a mother; proudly, like a father; eternally and unstintingly, as only God can love. He loves us wholly and completely, just as we are, and he longs to lavish his love upon us.

Some of us become aware of his love little by little, as a ray of light begins to penetrate a dark cellar, feebly at first, then growing and increasing until the whole cellar is illuminated. Others move instantly from darkness to light, like flowers leaning towards the sun when heavy clouds are suddenly banished. We come to realize his love is what we are searching for when we turn over one pleasure after another, seeking for the unknown thing that will revitalize us. His love is what we want when we move restlessly from lover to lover, from job to job, from town to town. His love is what makes our lives radiant with joyful meaning. God is all that is, and our thirsty spirits, at last making contact with him, rejoice with his disciples: "We have found the Lord!" (John 1:41).

TWO

The First Steps on the Spiritual Road

For a moment after our despairing cry to
God we seem to perceive a response, a
Presence veiled to our senses but revealed
to our spirit. We pause, listening, feeling
as if in the next moment we might escape
the limitations of our eyes and ears, and
see and speak with the Lord. Some people
report dramatic conversion experiences,
insisting that they see Christ physically and
hear his voice, but for most of us nothing
so dramatic happens exteriorly. God
doesn't appear in a cloud of trumpeting
cherubim. We are not raised to the third
heaven, like Paul, nor does God call to us
from a burning bush, as he did to Moses.

The moment passes, the Presence seems no longer there. We shake our heads and return to "reality," but the awareness that we have called to God with our whole being persists. The very intensity of our call puzzles us. We have been taught for years that things of the spirit are beyond the reach of the senses. Better watch that religious stuff! Aware of an invisible Presence, indeed! Maybe we are getting soft in the head.

THE HIDDEN GOD

Hidden! Why is God so hidden? Lord, why won't you show your face to me, just once, to help my unbelief? I want to believe in you. I want to love you, to do your will. But how can I love you when I cannot see or hear you, cannot touch you, cannot even find you?

Why does God maintain such a low profile that we can go days, weeks, years without giving him more than a cursory thought? How can we know this hidden God? Where do we find him? How can we love him? It's impossible!

Yes. For us, impossible. Jesus himself says so. "It was not you who chose me," he tells us. "It was I who chose you" (John 15:16).

Well, that puts the ball squarely in God's court! We're off the hook. Back to football and the soaps on television, and let the souls God "chooses" take care of the spiritual life! As for that moment when we called on him—that must have been an emotional aberration, a reversion to childhood dreams of a God who provides us with unending happiness. Not that we take back the call, exactly. We just don't believe anything will come of it.

Not so fast. There's a rider. God chooses us all. No exceptions.

He loves each and every one of us, in spite of the barricades we raise against his love. He dwells within us, as near to us as our own heart and soul: "The reign of God is already in your midst," Jesus says (Luke 17:21). But we have not learned to seek or find him within us. It is as if we had confined him, like an unwelcome guest, to a single room far from the center of the house, a room whose door we never allow to be opened. Now we have opened that door and invited him to take possession of us.

Imagine the joy of an overprotective mother called to her daughter-in-law's house in a crisis. With what energetic delight she straightens out the closets, organizes the bureaus, irons her son's shirts just the way he likes them, and fills the freezer with her own good meals, enough to last for many days after she returns to her own house.

She works feverishly to set everything in good order while her invitation to do so remains in effect. Her mark will remain on her son's household after she is gone. Her standards of order may even take hold.

GOD ACTS WITHIN US

St. Teresa of Jesus, in her book *The Way of Perfection*, suggests we imagine "that we have within us a most splendid palace . . . and we are partly responsible for the condition of this building." God responds to our invitation to take greater possession of our interior castle, and what does he find? An architect's nightmare, with ells tacked on here and chimneys crumbling there, the whole edifice falling into the ground from neglect; the lawns overgrown with weeds and brambles; the trees and shrubs in need of feeding and pruning. Our bodies are abused by the poisons we use to relieve tension; our spirits trammeled by anxieties; the whole defended by a strongly aggressive psychological structure bent on excessive concern for itself. There is so much to set right that only God would know where to begin.

Hardly a fit dwelling for a King! But he accepts the miserable accomodations we offer him. Quietly, graciously, he begins to set things in order, to restore the splendor of the soul he created. His touch is as delicate as a flurry of snowflakes that falls in the night, to be swept away by the wind before morning. Nothing remains but a certain fresh scent in the air to show that snow has fallen, yet a change has taken place.

At first we are unaware of God's action within us. Expecting him to be Santa Claus, we relate to God in a very primitive fashion, demanding good things of him like spoiled children crying for candy. "Lord, we need a better place to live. God, please give my husband a better job. God, our car is falling apart. Lord, why can't we have a vacation house?"

Gimme, gimme, gimme. If you would only do what I ask, Lord, oh, how I would believe in you!

God is not insensitive to our cries, but he has better things to give us than those we are asking for. Before we can enjoy these gifts, we must be gently remolded to our original shape, to the creature God saw as his creation from all eternity. Our taste for the things of God has been blunted, our appetites spoiled. From much brushing with evil, we have taken on something of the tastes and appearance of the prince of darkness and must be restored to our original beauty as children of light.

Before we can love God, we must know him, and he begins to draw us closer to him. At first his pull may be hardly noticeable: we pass a chapel during our shopping spree and drop in on the spur of the moment, wondering at ourselves as we do so. The visit may be only seconds long, just time for the briefest of aspirations: "Lord, have mercy on me." We might even kneel for a moment, with mixed feelings of skepticism and bemusement at finding ourselves there. It may be the first time in our lives that we have dropped into church when we didn't have to. God is drawing us.

Perhaps a reading at Mass suddenly gives us a totally different image of Christ. Jesus has always been portrayed as a gentle figure—in worldly affairs, even an ineffective one. He wore a long robe that in spite of ourselves carries for us an image of effeminacy. Suddenly we hear him defying the Pharisees and realize, "Why, Christ was a rebel!" We start to see him in a new light. Those were fishermen he called, and fishermen are hardly the type to sit about drinking tea and exclaiming, "Heavens to Betsy!" So much for the long robe.

Perhaps the Lord gives consolation in prayer, a sense of his closeness, of his love and understanding that makes us want to experience more of it. If we respond to his gentle invitations, he will issue them more regularly. Although we are still far from sanctity, we begin to think of him more often and we try harder to please him.

CHRIST, THE GOOD SHEPHERD

Sheep are stupid creatures. They don't know enough to move from a grazed-out spot to a grassy one until the shepherd leads them there. They wander off and get stuck in hedges and holes. They fall over and can't get to their feet unaided; the shepherd must rescue them and set them upright or they will remain on their backs, easy prey for wolves. About the only thing to be said for sheep is that they know their shepherd's voice and will follow no other.

Christ didn't call himself the Good Shepherd for nothing. We, like sheep, go our own shortsighted way, failing to find food, falling into ditches, unable to right ourselves when we fall. But unlike them, when we hear our shepherd calling us in a direction we would rather not go, we hesitate to follow him.

God leads us, like sheep, on the first steps of the spiritual road. That road begins in a broad and easy place, but it leads up a steep and rugged mountain. Many, many people turn aside as soon as the ascent begins to tell on their weak spiritual muscles, and remain all their earthly lives on the grassy levels where the way is easy.

Christ doesn't force us to follow. He will still love us if we remain behind where the road is broad and smooth. He will love us if we choose comfort, convenience, and selfish desires over his company. But he will not reveal himself in the same way as he does to those who follow him whole-heartedly.

We follow Christ by being faithful to prayer and by obeying those inner impulses that prompt us to acts of love or faith. Perhaps we find ourselves unexpectedly free at an hour when we could go to Mass and it isn't even Sunday. Follow his prompting and go. You won't feel like a saint. In fact you might feel a little foolish, especially when a neighbor teases, "Didn't I see you going into church this morning? What's going on—are you getting holy, or something?"

It is a long way from these first steps to being holy, but God is working in us. The more closely we respond, the faster the work goes. "Souls have no idea what I would work in them," he told St. Margaret Mary Alacoque, "if only they didn't resist me."

The Lord will prompt us to little acts of love, so small we can't possibly take pride in them. We want to crow, "I told you so!" when one of our children is snubbed by a schoolmate. But instead, seeing that subdued, chastened look behind the bravado, we speak as a supportive parent, saying only, "How disappointing for you." Or a woman behind us in the supermarket checkout line with two tired, cranky children is obviously anxious to get home, and we, usually to our own great surprise, volunteer to let her go ahead of us. That's God at work.

Understand that during this time when we surprise ourselves with little acts of patience and kindness God still seems far away, remote, a myth, a wonderful story we wish had more reality for us. Where are the miracles he promised us? "I assure you, if you had faith the size of a mustard seed, you would be able to say to this mountain, 'Move from here to there,' and it would move. Nothing would be impossible for you" (Matthew 17:20). And again: "If you had faith the size of a mustard seed, you could say to this sycamore, 'Be uprooted and transplanted into the sea,' and it would obey you" (Luke 17:6). "I solemnly assure you, the man who has faith in me will do the works I do, and greater far than these. Why? Because I go to the Father" (John 14:12).

Greater miracles than Christ performed? Sure. Meanwhile let's get the groceries put away and dinner on the table, and don't think too hard about spiritual things or it will make you dizzy.

Even as we shy away from thinking of spiritual matters, God is doing great things within us, miracles only he can perform. He is softening our stony hearts and taking down the defenses we have erected against loving in order to protect our own self-love. He presents us with opportunities on all sides to cooperate in this work of learning to love others rather than self, to overcome our defensiveness, our hurt pride, our selfishness. We don't always recognize these opportunities. In fact, it may seem that the world is dumping on us more than ever.

A SAINT'S EXAMPLE

St. Therese of Lisieux, the Little Flower, recounts her first victory over self in her autobiography, *Story of a Soul*. Therese entered Carmel at fifteen and since she was the youngest in the house, everything that went wrong was blamed on her. One day the mistress of novices found a jar somebody had broken and tried to hide behind a window covering. At once she accused Therese, who just as promptly rallied to defend herself. Then God took over. She realized that he was presenting her with an opportunity to grow in mastery of self. Instead of defending herself, she kissed the ground and promised to do better in future.

Was it easy? No. "I was so little advanced in perfection," Therese admits, "that even trifles like these cost me dear."

Knocking down the walls of our self-love is never easy. On the contrary, it is so difficult that whenever we achieve a victory, we know it is only because God is helping us. We cannot do it on our own.

Why let others blame us for things that aren't our fault? Why not speak up when we're stepped on? When somebody shoves ahead of us in line, surely it is only human to get angry! Why should we pretend otherwise?

We shouldn't pretend. There is a difference between suppression, which is knowing what we are feeling but choosing not to act on it, and repression, which is denying our feelings to ourselves. The latter leads to psychological and emotional ills and to a false way of behaving, which is the last thing God wants.

God removes our self-love and replaces it, not with repression, but with love of others. He gives us great interior freedom and an inner sense of profound security that we can't give ourselves or get from the world, a security whose depth astonishes us.

God is still hidden, but our interior landscape is starting to thrive under his gentle care. On the outside there are no signs or wonders. Prayer may still be an arid experience, often still no more than "saying prayers." But even saying prayers is an indication of our good will and desire to please God, a preparation for the experience of prayer that he will give us if we desire it and are faithful to him. And we do desire it. We want to know our Lord better. He himself gives us the desire. We are starting to grow spiritually in little ways, just putting forth the tiniest of buds, while God is strengthening and preparing us for a major step in the spiritual life.

ACCEPTING GOD'S WILL

Christ promised that he and the Father would come and dwell with those who loved him and he would reveal himself to them (John 14:23). He keeps his promise. If we have not discovered him in ourselves, not felt that we are growing in knowledge of him, we may have overlooked a very important prerequisite. That prerequisite is that we must love him, and he gave us a yardstick for measuring this love: "He who obeys the commandments he has from me is the man who loves me" (John 14:21).

Again: "Love me and obey the command I give you" (John 14:14).

We have always known the commandments and have tried to keep them, but we begin to understand that loving God isn't simply a matter of doing this and avoiding that, checking sins off in one column and virtues in another. We come to understand that loving God means referring to him in all we do in order to follow the way Christ taught us, the way of love. To keep God's commandments means to live in the will of God, not in our own.

Unless we are committing the most atrocious sins, we think we *are* doing God's will. We even say now and then, "God willing," and "Whatever God wills." We may even pray to do his will. We certainly say the Our Father frequently, including the plea that, "Thy will be done."

Have you ever caught yourself at these prayers?

"Lord, whatever you will. Please don't ever let me have cancer."

"Lord, whatever you will. Please take care of us financially. I couldn't stand being really poor."

"Lord, whatever you will. Please don't take my parents yet."

29

What we're saying is, Lord, whatever *I* will.

If we are serious about living a Christian life, we become ever more sensitive to following God's inner promptings. When we begin following his lead, sooner or later we come to realize that we are not in tune with his will at all. In fact, we are afraid of it. We see our lives in a nearsighted, self-loving way. We anticipate the rewards and pleasures of life: promotions, good marriages for our children, healthy grandchildren, an old age full of comfort and honor. And we say, "Your will, Lord," with the reservation that he shouldn't desire anything contrary to what we desire.

Suppose he desires to bring home to himself the person I love most. Will I still say so glibly, "Your will, Lord?" What if I lose everything I have accumulated and end my days on welfare? What if I have a grandchild who is autistic? Do I really mean, "Your will, Lord?"

The answer is, we don't. Yet until we do mean what we say, desiring his will and not our own, we make no progress in the spiritual life. The desire for his will to supercede our own, *in all things*, is the most critical step on the interior journey.

Oh, how we cling to our wills! Our me-firstness that shows itself in outrage over little slights, in getting there first with the most, in beating out the other guy so the world can see how wonderful we are. How we cling to our common sense, which assures us we can insure our health and comfort by subscribing to the right medical plan, going after the job with the best fringe benefits, and preparing financially for the future.

Because we are trying in good faith to please God, we become aware that by clinging to our own puny wills, to our good common sense, we are trying to control the circumstances of our lives. We cling to a false security because we don't know God well enough to trust him fully. A little thought will show us that only God can insure our health. Only he can insure our future. If we fall ill for a long time, we come to realize very quickly that our health is in the hands of God. If fortune goes against us, we begin to think seriously about our limitations. And when we lose loved ones, we realize that life and death are not under our control at all.

God is our Creator. He made us in love and redeemed us in love. He loves us perfectly and infinitely. How could anything he desires be less good for us than what we desire for ourselves? Do we trust the God who died for us enough to surrender ourselves into his hand?

The truth is, we don't trust him yet. We are still too new in the spiritual life to know, with every fiber of our being, that God alone is never-failing in his concern for us. The idea of yielding conscious control over our lives scares us. Yet God seems to desire this yielding from us as a measure of our trust in him, and trust is a measure of our love.

We must beg God to teach us to trust him. His providence is all around us. The sun comes up every day, rain falls to nourish our crops, but we can't translate God's general providence into his loving concern for us as individuals. Although we know Christ died for us—for me!—we still falter when it comes to surrendering our life to him. But because we do want to follow him, we do want to please him, he leads us step by step to the place in the road where this surrender must be made if we are ever to reach the heights, rather than remain on the broad and grassy path at the base of the mountain.

THE INITIAL SURRENDER

The more clearly we see the need, the greater our desire to yield. We pray for the grace to do so, for something in us hesitates at the thought of surrender.

Sometimes God helps us by letting us see how false the values of the world are. We become more and more convinced that only spiritual values last. We come to an understanding that knowing and loving God is the great adventure and something in us wants to get on with it even while we balk.

We try to pray without qualifications. "Your will, Lord." What if he means to let me become blind? We counter such fears by telling ourselves God is love. Christ died for us. If he allows such a calamity, it is only because he knows what is best for us. What child doesn't turn away from bitter medicine? Looking at life in our narrow, earthbound way, we cannot see how sometimes unpleasant things may do us more good than the pleasures we want. So we manage to say, in fear and trembling, "Your will, Lord," and try to squelch the rider: "But please don't let anything bad happen to me." We pray for the grace to accept his will unconditionally, and one day, because he loves us, the grace is given. We say, "Your will, Lord," consciously submitting ourselves to his will with no qualifications.

That initial surrender is like plunging into cold water from a high cliff. That actual moment of falling, with no support, is not easy. Knowing so little of love ourselves, having made the initial surrender, we expect the King of Love to act like a tyrant, to strike us dumb and paralyzed in the next instant, to send our house up in flames, to destroy our loved ones in an accident.

In short, we expect God to act like the devil.

How little we know him! Yet we will soon know him intimately, experience his unfailing goodness and ever-present love. In time we will smile over the fearful, ignorant creature who came so hesitantly and so anxiously to his Lord.

Yet in with the act of yielding, we feel momentarily empty, as if the goblet of self had spilled out its last bit of liquid on the sand. And how bitter that liquid is! We wait patiently, not knowing where or how or even if we are ever to be filled again.

But here comes the sea, rushing in upon the goblet, catching it up and filling it full and overfull and overflowing with itself, making it part of itself. In a blaze of transcendent joy, we realized that God means to fill us with himself, to carry us in himself as the sea carries the goblet.

The work of transformation has begun.

THREE

Opening Ourselves to God

One of the first things that happens after
we offer God our will is that prayer starts
to attract us. We make time for it at the
expense of other activities. At first, the best
we might do is squeeze in a few extra
minutes at the end of a crowded day. God
has been so accustomed to receiving almost
no attention from us, however, that he
accepts this poor beginning graciously. As
we persevere, we realize that God prefers
prime time, and we start reordering our
schedules to give him an hour when we are
at our best.

Who would have thought that God would
win over the movie channel? That we

would willingly—eagerly!—leave a party early to spend time talking to him? Until we open ourselves unstintingly to God's action, everything seems to attract us more than being with him. Now we regret our previous neglect, for we see we have wasted much of our lives on things that have no lasting value, for they do not bring us to God.

At first we may be shy about our growing attraction to prayer, embarrassed at the thought of being caught praying. We find the biblical admonition to go to our room and close the door easy to follow (Matthew 6:6). God our Father is indeed in that secret place, and he does reward us.

Our prayer becomes refreshing. Even on days when we have to push ourselves to begin our daily hour, we find that perseverence pays, and we come forth from that hour with greater peace in our hearts and a growing confidence that God is near and cares intensely about us. Yet we are hesitant to speak of our relationship with God, as though it were an unforgiveable *faux pas* akin to broadcasting our most intimate secrets. Our very embarrassment embarrasses us for we begin to see what a poor return we give God for his goodness to us, a goodness that daily becomes more recognizable.

At the same time we are afraid of our new interest in prayer. Saints liked to pray.

Does our growing enjoyment of prayer mean we might wind up saints? That's heavy! In general our idea of sanctity is as wide of the mark as our idea of God, but having made our initial surrender to his will we declare ourselves willing, with many a shudder and bouts of fearfulness, to let God make us a saint, if that is what he wants. Fortunately, for most of us it takes many years, and the first panic that he will do something startling, "Go, my child, to the president, and tell him in my name . . ., "wears off as we come to know him better.

Now we understand Jonah's reluctance to follow God's call to preach at Nineveh, knowing that the sophisticates of that city would laugh at him. It was only after he tried to run from God and was delivered from the large fish that he obeyed (Jonah 3:3). Once we thought him a spineless clod. Now we can sympathize, for what if God should say to us, "Up! Go to New York and preach to them as I told you!" Surely we would run too even though we have told God we desire his will in everything.

We can appreciate Moses reminding God of his stammer when Yahweh proposed to send him to the great king, Pharaoh: "Since I am a poor speaker, how can it be that Pharaoh will listen to me?" God knew that Moses was slow of speech, but Moses was the one he had chosen to be his prophet. The difficulty was resolved by having Aaron, Moses' brother, repeat to Pharaoh what Moses told him to say.

Like the prophets, we too see our weaknesses and wonder how God means to circumvent them, for as we grow in prayer we see what poor creatures we are and how much healing must be done to make us whole.

IN LOVE WITH GOD

God loves us, and we begin to fall in love with him. Little by little, God, who was only a word to us, a myth, a fantasy figure, becomes real. In prayer we feel his presence. He is sometimes so near we feel we can almost touch him physically. At each meeting, we come to know him better. He envelops us in his love. Just as a meeting with a human lover leaves us glowing, so too the meeting with our divine lover leaves its mark. The words of the prophet Jeremiah sink deeply, "You have seduced me, O Yahweh, and I have let myself be seduced" (Jeremiah 20:7).

When we first come to true prayer, God treats us like the spiritual infants we are and makes it delightful. We emerge from prayer as from a refreshing bath, renewed and ready to tackle the problems of life with increased zest. Sometimes he fills us with a giddy joy similar to the heady exhilaration that accompanies an earthbound tryst. We understand the exuberance of the apostles, so filled with the joy of the Holy Spirit at Pentecost that onlookers thought they must have been drinking, although it was only nine o'clock in the morning (Acts 2:13–15).

With God, we never reach bottom. We continue to fall ever deeper in love without discovering all there is to him. Although we are to live forever and to share eternity with him, we will never come to the end of him. Soon after realizing this we are moved to gratitude. What wonderful luck to discover God while we are still on earth! It gives us a head start on the joys of heaven. And to think we have wasted years all bound up in our small finite self, when we might have been getting to know him! We have begun to experience prayer for what it is, not a numbing repetition of meaningless words, but a love exchange between God and the soul.

SOME EFFECTS OF PRAYER

When we come to prayer, our body still manifests its feelings and physical needs and restrictions. As if to convince us of the reality of spiritual gifts the senses cannot apprehend, the joy of falling in love with the Creator seems to overflow into the body. We feel loved. We feel treasured, comforted, at peace. The floor is as hard under our knees as it always was, and our backs get stiff from kneeling as they always did, but these small discomforts no longer terminate our prayer prematurely. Indeed, we feel a growing desire to tame the body's excessive demands. We realize our own comfort must not be allowed to impede us as we reach out to God in prayer.

If we remain faithful, the day will come when we are so caught up by God our prayer time will seem too short, for now when we pray we know ourselves to be with our perfect lover and we cling to him with all our might.

SOLITUDE AND SILENCE

God, who dwells within us, leads us to withdraw within ourselves to be with him. Although we may resist at first, in time we come to desire this solitude as a contrast to our active lives.

Wanting to be alone in this day and age has pathological overtones. It is considered antisocial at best and psychotic at worst. But God doesn't draw us inward to sever our ties with friends and family, but rather to strengthen them with his love. When our relationship with him is cemented in solitude, he turns us out again to spread his light and love in the world.

If we have never been able to stay alone before, our developing taste for solitude surprises us. In our life before prayer we felt lonely when we were alone. Now we are not really alone, but with God. His company makes all the difference.

If desiring solitude is thought strange, preferring silence is considered downright peculiar. We live in a noisy world. Traffic, power tools, and stereos are a constant background. Jet airplanes, vacuum cleaners, and dishwashers add their disharmony. If these don't drive out silence completely enough, wear headphones when you go jogging! Satan forbid that you should have the quiet to meet the God dwelling within you.

We are so used to noise we don't realize how it bruises until God leads us to the desert and speaks to our hearts (Hosea 2:16). We learn that silence isn't loneliness. It isn't lifelessness. It isn't death. Silence is rather the antechamber of prayer, a place we visit often on our spiritual journey, with ever-growing eagerness for the repose we find there. It refreshes us for our return to the hurly-burly of life.

ADVANCING IN PRAYER

Prayer itself takes on a vitality we seldom, perhaps never, experienced in the past.

Scripture tells us that we do not know how to pray as we ought to, so the Spirit intercedes for us (Romans 8:26). Certainly we find a rhythm and a life to prayer that we were unaware of.

We no longer merely recite words or rattle off a list of complaints, and call that prayer. We might begin our prayer time with complaints, or by reading favorite prayers, but now we know this is only a preliminary activity to the main event. As we wait on God, he stills us and brings us to silence, a silence in which he is present. We become lost in him.

Or perhaps we begin in silence, meditating on one of the mysteries of the rosary. In meditation we use our mind and imagination to picture to ourselves an event in the life of Christ. He may fill us with such joy we cannot be still and we erupt in words of praise—vocal prayer, true prayer, for the heart is involved and the mind lifted to God.

As we come hour by hour to a deeper knowledge and love of God, we are filled with praise for his glory. We find ourselves making spontaneous acts of adoration, for we see his glory all around us in the beauty and grandeur of nature and see how little we are in comparison with the Creator. Our prayers of love increase, for we sense a growing peace and joy and a new attitude toward life's difficulties. Trifles that once kept us in turmoil and self-pity now are simply that—trifles. We sense the helping hand of God in everything that falls to us and wonder anew at the mystery of his love. Love leads to contrition and to gratitude, and our prayers of petition are now balanced with more frequent acts of adoration, thanksgiving, and love.

The nature of our petitions changes. Whereas before we prayed mainly for material things, calling on God with a certain desperation as if he didn't know who we were or what our situation was, now we ask for other gifts. For the ability to love him and others. For deeper faith. For the advance of his Kingdom. For all hearts to be drawn to him. That he might come again, soon, and claim us. For peace and love among all the people on earth. That his name might be glorified.

We continue to pray for material things as well. He wants us to do so because he delights in giving, and even more in our acknowledgment of him as giver. Yet now we pray realizing that he knows and understands the situation exactly, with all of its ramifications past, present, and into infinity. We know that he loves each of us more than we possibly can love one another so we are less inclined to tell him how to handle things.

Instead of praying, "God, please cure Michael," we find ourselves saying, "Lord, Michael, whom you love, is suffering very much. It's not only the physical aspects; he's worried about his family because he can no longer work. I know that in your great love you will take care of him."

It is no longer necessary to twist God's arm by trying to tell him what is best. He knows what is best—physical healing, spiritual healing, ability to grow in understanding and compassion—and we know that he will do what is best.

GOD IN CREATION

We know we are advancing in spirituality by our growth in faith and in love. The more we love, the closer we are to God. Conversely, the closer we become to God, the more we love. We realize in truth that we are brother and sister to all human beings, for all were created by God our Father and redeemed by Christ. We feel connected to all that God has made in the physical world as well. The world becomes our textbook, a shadow and symbol of the spiritual world.

A snail tumbles, fully extended, in the waves, and the thought comes: that is how we should open ourselves to God, fully, fearlessly, allowing him to move us in whatever direction he chooses, while we are fed and nourished by him.

The sky is overcast for the third straight day, and it seems as if the sun will never shine again. And we think, yes, when things are dark in our lives it seems that God has disappeared. We look, and cannot find him. But just as the sun is there, hidden, still warming the earth, God is there also, unseen, his love sustaining us. The clouds will pass and the sun will reappear. This darkness will pass, and the light of Christ will flood my life once again.

Everything he has created trembles with mystery. This six-foot-four man with a thick beard was once an infant who fit in my hand. How do you change infants into adults, Lord?

How is it the earth, this dirt, sends up fruit and flowers? God, how did you ever think of daffodils? What gave you the idea for changing the seasons, Lord? How did you think of the sea? The words of the psalmist strike us forcefully, "When I behold your heavens, the work of your fingers, the moon and the stars which you set in place—What is man that you should be mindful of him; or the son of man that you should care for him?" (Psalm 8:4–5).

GOD IN THE COMMUNITY

In addition to drawing us to every place where he dwells—the eucharist, prayer, scripture, and spiritual reading—he draws

45

us into community. God leads us to other souls making the interior journey, for he knows a time will come when we must speak of him, just as infatuated people must speak of the beloved until others grow weary of listening. God knows we will need the support of human comfort. We need to share experiences and ask advice, and as the journey progresses we develop a hunger to pray with others. Nobody makes the spiritual journey alone.

God likes his friends to know one another, and he establishes spiritual friendships. These friendships have all the warmth of those we generate for ourselves, but none of the destructive passions, and they glow most warmly when the two friends speak of or to their Lord.

Christ himself encouraged praying together. He taught us to say "Our Father," rather than "My Father," and promised that, "Where two or three are gathered in my name, there am I in their midst" (Matthew 18:20).

The Curé of Ars had great esteem for community prayer. When a woman of a neighboring parish came to ask what she could do to help bring her parish back to spiritual ways, the Curé advised her to find one other person and pray together. After some months, he advised both to each find another person and for the four to pray together. When the group grew to twelve people coming together to pray for their parish, the pastor became aware of changes. His parish was revitalized spiritually and his people turned more and more completely to God.

The Curé himself preferred public to private prayers. "Private prayer," he used to say, "resembles straw scattered here and there over a field; if it is set on fire, the flame is not a powerful one; but if you gather those scattered straws into a bundle, the flame is bright, and rises in a lofty column towards the sky. Such is public prayer."

GOD IN THE LITURGY

The liturgy is the culmination of community prayer. We come together as one in answer to the prayer of Jesus to the Father, ". . . that they may be one, even as we are one" (John 17:11). The Mass becomes a shared feast of love: God's love for us, and ours for him and for one another.

Our prayer rises before him, not as single flames, but as a conflagration forcing back the darkness. The liturgy that in our days before prayer seemed so routine comes alive for us. Now the gospel reading is not about a remote figure, but news of our best friend whose life redeemed and gave value to our own. We have heard epistles and gospels so often that the familiarity of the words has blunted the story they tell. Now we listen with new ears as the readings strike us with a sense of wonder. We hear for what seems the first time the terrible frustration of Christ as he was met again and again with misunderstanding from his disciples and rejection from the people he had come to save, and we realize what great love fueled his mission.

While imprisoned in Jerusalem, Peter thought he dreamed that an angel freed him (Acts 12:6–11). The apostle becomes a real person to us as we relate to his astonishment when he discovers himself fully awake out on the streets. We see the boldness, inspired by love, of the woman who dared approach Christ in a strange house and wipe his feet with her hair (Luke 7:36–50). She was a woman of ill repute. How little Christ cared for such human standards! Rather than repudiate her, he praised her conduct as springing from great love and forgave her sins.

Once we were delighted when the priest skipped the homily. Now we feel cheated if this happens, for we are eager to hear more of the one who has captured our heart. Communion is no longer a matter of shuffling up the aisle with our minds on getting home before the pot roast is burned. Now we think of him and of sharing in the feast of love. We realize who it is that comes to us in the eucharist and we greet him with joy. Of this most intimate and precious time between God and the soul, St. Therese commented in her autobiography that, "I don't see what more I could have in heaven."

In the revelations Christ made to Sister Josefa Menendez, he told her that the eucharist is the invention of love. While he is present sacramentally, he longs to speak to those who have received him and longs to have them speak to him. All too often, however, he is received with hardly a thought, and his presence is dismissed from our consciousness in the time it takes us to return from the altar to the pew.

Now we welcome him with longing. Often, he grants us consolation at this time, renewing our faith and deepening our love. He continually increases our desire to know and love him more fully and to do whatever he desires of us.

THE COMMUNION OF SAINTS

We become increasingly aware that the road we have chosen, although close to the way of the world at its starting point, diverges ever more sharply from it. We lean for help on those who have traveled it before. Saints are no longer lifeless plaster statues, but real people who once started to climb by making the same choice that we have, to follow God's will rather than their own.

Their lives take on meaning for us. Grand saints in the tradition of stupendous miracles, great penances, and stigmata may raise only skepticism and a hope that God will draw us by a lesser way, but many saints had lives and problems that resemble our own: St. Rita, married to an alcoholic who drew their two sons into his own destructive ways; or St. Monica, a good Christian mother who prayed twenty long years for the conversion of her pagan son. The prayers worked. Her son was Augustine, one of the greatest saints of the church, whose prayer—"Lord, make me pure. But not yet!"—finds an echo in many a heart.

There is St. Therese, the Little Flower, who never had a vision in her life. She eschewed great physical penances in an age when they were thought to be necessary for great holiness and instead found the "little way" to sanctity. Offering up the noisy clacking of a sister's rosary beads that disturbed her own meditation. Volunteering to be the work partner of the sister who was so crochety and ill-natured that everybody's dearest wish was to avoid her. Eating moderately of every dish put before her. Mortifying her own tastes so completely that the nuns who lived in her convent didn't know which foods she liked or disliked. She knew very well it is not the magnitude of the work that matters, but the depth of love.

God opens our hearts. We see him everywhere and in all people. We feel united with every soul ever created, and a special love flows toward those living on earth with us now. We lose the need to appear great before them, to be recognized as somebody of importance. Love turns everything right-side up. We find ourselves choosing to serve our brothers and sisters rather than to be served; to praise rather than to criticize; to love in every way we can devise.

On this honeymoon period, as we live in love and in harmony with all around us, the soul in prayer knows itself to be with its Creator, and Christ is with the creature for whom he died. They gaze on one another like love-struck teenagers, not needing words to communicate perfectly. Now and again one might murmur, "My love, and the other answers, "Beloved," and their whole conversation consists in repetitions of the same, boring to distraction anyone who overhears, yet full of fascination for the lovers themselves, who cannot get enough of each other's company.

This embrace of God and the soul is prayer, and if you desire to experience it for yourself, ask him for it. God wants us to come to him freely, knowing everything we might have chosen instead of him and freely and joyfully consigning it to the trash can. He is all that is. Having come to him, our only regret will be that we did not respond to his invitation sooner.

FOUR

Growing Closer to God

As we grow in prayer, we realize how little
of our previous prayer was worthy of the
name. Rather than a meeting in love with
our God, the source of all love, our past
prayer was more a series of challenges to
an unknown computer in the sky. Prove
that you're there, God, and then I'll think
about doing things your way! Show me
you exist by setting things right according
to my lights. Come down from the cross,
and then I'll believe you. Like the
unbelievers at the crucifixion, our prayer
was, "He saved others but he cannot save
himself!" (Matthew 27:42, Mark 15:32, Luke
23:35).

The people who insisted Christ leave the cross weren't simply jeering. Those who followed the law of Moses in good faith believed firmly in one God, a God so holy that his name was never spoken. To believe in Christ, who claimed to be the redeemer spoken of in the scriptures, was idolatry to them. They *needed* proof.

The Pharisees reminded Christ that Moses had fed the Israelites with manna from heaven in the desert. Let him work a sign in the sky, and then they would believe (Matthew 16:1, Luke 11:29), but Jesus denied emphatically the request for a sign. "An evil, faithless age is eager for a sign, but no sign will be given it except that of Jonah!" (Matthew 16:4). His resurrection after three days in the tomb would be the sign. One assumes the Pharisees left him, mumbling to themselves that if Jesus were really the Messiah, he would have worked something in the heavens without thinking twice about it. Maybe cause the sun to stand still, as it did for Hezekiah, a faithful servant of God, as a sign that God would lengthen his life and spare him and his people from the hands of the Assyrians (2 Kings 20:1–11). Perhaps let the sun throw off many colors and seem to plunge to earth, as it was to do at Fatima. If Jesus wasn't willing, or able, to do a little thing like that, then why should they believe in him?

After we come to real prayer, we experience a continual deepening of faith. Our belief, which at best was soft as a sponge, begins to grow firm until, like the faith of Peter, it is a rock (Matthew 16:18).

When Christ arrived at the home of Martha and Mary, who had buried their brother Lazarus four days previously, Martha said, "Lord, if you had been here, my brother would never have died." She didn't ask Christ to restore him to life. She simply said with complete faith, "Even now, I am sure that God will give you whatever you ask of him" (John 11:21, 22).

Christ went to the tomb and called Lazarus forth.

It's a funny thing, but even when we see miracles we don't believe them. Lazarus comes forth from the tomb. Everybody is overwhelmed. News spreads. Then the skeptics get to work.

"He wasn't dead. It was a put-up job. They want to make that preacher Jesus a king. People have been sneaking into the tomb feeding Lazarus secretly. Let's look at this thing rationally. If Jesus can really raise people from the dead, why doesn't he raise David? Or Moses? Give us back our great patriarchs! Make us a great nation! Free us from the Roman yoke!"

God's ways are not ours. As faith grows, we measure what we see with a new yardstick, judging events in the light of eternity rather than solely in the here-and-now. Even when we don't understand why a given thing happens, we continue to grow in the assurance that God's way is best.

LOSS OF FEAR

Christ promised that those who have ". . . given up home, brothers or sisters, father or mother, wife or children or property for my sake will receive many times as much and inherit everlasting life" (Matthew 19:29). Even without so great a renunciation on our part, God begins to reward our early efforts to please him.

As we begin to trust his love, the first reward is that our image of him as a despot driven by whims disappears forever. "Love has no room for fear," scripture tells us. "Perfect love casts out all fear. And since fear has to do with punishment, love is not yet perfect in one who is afraid" (1 John 4:18).

The second reward is that we lose our fear of hell. Hell is the place where no love exists. Here on earth we feel in ourselves the desire to love God more and more. We cannot imagine ever denying our love of God, nor can we imagine God ceasing to love us. "God is love, and he who abides in love abides in God, and God in him" (1 John 4:16).

As we lose the fear of hell, we lose the fear of death and all the anxiety that surrounds aging and sickness. Death becomes nothing more than the final trysting place where God and the soul meet. Thus aging can become a joyful process, for it assures us we are approaching that meeting. Sickness becomes a way of offering a little discomfort back in love for the great suffering Christ took on for us.

Not only do we lose our fear of sickness and death, but of all forms of suffering. Suffering is one of the forfeits we won when we turned away from God. Now, instead of blaming him for our pain, we realize that if he had not redeemed us, we would all know a great deal more suffering.

No normal person likes to suffer. Even the saints didn't enjoy it, but only used suffering to bring themselves closer to God. If we can endure suffering as an act of love and reparation, it helps allay our fear of it.

When we are helpless, at the mercy of pain and the ministrations of others, we seem to develop a finer appreciation of our littleness. We who would be masters of the world, who would reach the stars and harness the wind and waves to our bidding, become aware that we cannot even control our next breath. Often that awareness sharpens our ears to hear the voice of God.

We no longer fear the physical process of dying, not even of dying alone because we know so firmly that God is with us. As we progress along the spiritual road, we become so assured of continuing life and come to such a degree of love for God that the long separation of earthly life becomes trying, and we yearn for the moment when we can lay our life down and embrace God in heaven forever.

St. Teresa of Jesus likened life on earth to a night in a miserable inn, and the person surrendered to God comes to complete agreement with her. While the mysteries of the physical world entrance us and its beauty becomes more and more stunning, we realize that this is only a shadow of the beauty and majesty of God, and our longing to see him as he is and to be with him forever grows like fire and sets the soul aflame with desire.

No matter how greatly we love God, our love remains small and finite, limited on all sides by our self-interest and littleness. God's love for us is infinite, unlimited, never-ending. When we think of who it is loving us—the Creator of all that is, the Being who alone owes existence to no one, the Source of all love, goodness, and knowledge—we grow in longing to return to him. This very growth of love destroys in its train all fear of physical suffering. Only one fear takes root in its place—that we might in our foolishness turn from him and offend him mortally, losing him forever. We beg God fervently never to let us be separated from him, never to let us for the least second slip out of his hand.

GETTING TO KNOW OURSELVES

As God gives us a deeper knowledge of himself, he also gives us deeper self-knowledge. We begin to see ourselves with his eyes and the view isn't always pretty. We discover faults and failings we had not been aware of. This doesn't happen in a negative, self-defeating way, but in a spirit of acceptance and love for ourselves as his creatures. If we have had an exaggerated idea of our importance, he begins to correct it. If, on the other hand, we have valued ourselves too little or felt ourselves worthless and without accomplishment, we begin to see ourselves in his eyes, as creatures worthy of love. At the same time we see clearly that we are truly nothing, a handful of dust given significance only by God creating and dwelling within us, and we are moved anew to wonder how God so great could love his creatures, who seem to love everything and everyone but him.

That he should have become one with us
and died for us is a mystery impossible to
encompass. "How good of God to
command us to love Him," St. Therese
writes in her autobiography, "For if he had
not commanded it, how should we dare?"

LIVING IN HIS LOVE

God's unconditional love for us inspires
growing confidence in him. This
confidence spills over into everyday life
and demolishes our fears and anxieties. We
feel ourselves living in his hand, so to
speak. We can tear ourselves away if we
wish, but he will never cast us out.

From this confidence comes a kind of
indifference to whatever life may bring. If
riches and good health, so be it. If poverty
and illness, so be it. God is with us in
everything. Everything becomes only
another setting in which the dialogue of
love goes on.

This is not to say that we should sit back,
do nothing, and expect God to live our
lives for us. He created us in freedom with
free wills and varying degrees of ability.
He set us in the material world to grow in
love of him and one another by exercising
our talents and using the means and
opportunities offered by the world.

He knows the circumstances of our lives
and our daily responsibilities, and it is in

carrying them out that we please him. Some people have the mistaken idea that praying means running off to church for hours on end. Fine, if you are free to do so. But if you have a job or a home or relatives to care for, it is by doing that job well, running that home efficiently, and caring for your family with loving kindness that you honor God and scale the heights of sanctity.

God teaches us to live in the present moment. Living in his will is the culmination of prayer and it takes a long while to be able to do so constantly. If his will for you at this moment is to be cooking chicken and squash, then doing so to the best of your ability is the finest gift you could give him and it is sanctifying as well. He will give you opportunities to get to church and speak to him there. When he calls you to church, and you obey, then that is living in his will; but to run to church when he desires you to be tending to the home, or conversely, to be tending to other things when he calls you to church, is once more doing our will and not his.

It takes a lifetime to learn to live in a manner of complete surrender to his will. We have begun this way of life by our initial surrender. Day by day he makes us more pliant, more sensitive to his desires.

Yielding to him brings us to the serenity exemplified by St. Francis's famous prayer: "Lord, grant me the serenity to accept the things I cannot change, the courage to change the things I can, and the wisdom to know the difference."

ABOUT OUR FATHER'S BUSINESS

One of the things we cannot change is other people. In the first flush of our growing awareness of God and our joy in him, we sometimes behold ourselves in an aura of holiness that owes more to imagination than to reality. In our delight at coming to know God better, we often desire the whole world to come closer to him too. There is nothing wrong with the desire. Yet often, in our immature zeal, we become judges of the spiritual state of those around us—a state that no one can judge but God.

We want to bring back straying relatives to the Church. We wish our parents weren't so materialistic. Our siblings don't pray enough. Our children are too enmeshed in worldly activities. Our co-workers are practically heathens. And in a fine spirit of charity, we think, we go about preaching to everybody, instructing them how to become holy like our humble selves and how to live their lives to please God better.

Our words have unexpected effects. Most

people run the other way when they see a self-appointed "holy teacher" coming. Those who seemed merely indifferent to spiritual things become angry and defiant at being told how to live—and with good reason. Yet even when their words do not have the desired results, the zealous ones continue to preach. Many, many good people think they are doing God's work by chastising others, when in effect they are only giving their own egos a boost.

If you are truly concerned about the spiritual lives of those close to you, pray for them. Your words may never bring an errant relative back to the sacraments, but your prayers and good example will. The more your relative resists, the harder you pray, without broadcasting the fact. In really stubborn cases, small sacrifices help. Make sure that they are small enough to raise no pride in you, and that they don't discommode anyone but yourself. Be loving in all circumstances and do not trumpet your little kindnesses before others. Your prayers and sacrifices will touch the heart of God, who loves your loved ones far more than you can. In response to your prayers, he will give them the grace to return to him.

The touchstone of growth in prayer is not delight in prayer, or new insight into scripture, or a desire to buttonhole everyone within hearing and tell them of

God. It is love. Quite soon along the road God teaches us to hold everything we do or intend to do up to a single question: Is this loving? All too often the answer is no.

Telling people they are spiritual ignoramuses, no matter how plainly their lives may seem to indicate no spiritual values whatever, is not in the least loving. It is pride, nothing more. The Holy Spirit is the Teacher, the Source of wisdom, the one who instructs us in all things of God, and if you think he has appointed you to speak for him, close yourself up in your room and pray about it for at least a hundred years.

But "faith comes through hearing" (Romans 10:17), and how can sinners hear if no one speaks?

If God wants you to speak for him, he usually makes that plain in a very definite, everyday fashion: *the other person asks you about him*, without prompting on your part. Until then your good example and secret prayers should suffice. When you are asked, it won't be because you have been flaunting your knowledge, but because you have been living the life of supernatural love. It is love that draws people to God, and they are not fooled by counterfeits. Love was the mark of the early Christians. Love drew others to follow their way, and love will draw people today.

If you still harbor a liking for gossip, for instance, you still have a way to go. As God draws us farther along the way of love, gossip becomes so painful we can't bring ourselves to speak a single word of it or to listen to it, even though at one time gossip might have been our favorite pastime. God is sensitizing us to become loving, as he is. Talk that deflates other people is so unloving it hurts.

On a snowy day do we take the parking place a neighbor has shoveled out and gloat at our cleverness? We still have a way to go. Do we buy goods at a sale price at one store and return them to another for full price? Do we dump work we find distasteful on a meeker colleague? Bring home supplies from the office for our own use? Cheat on taxes?

In these cases, we still have plenty of work to do on ourselves without setting ourselves up to preach to others.

BEING IN THE RIGHT PLACE

Although our early zeal may be misplaced, the desire to advance the kingdom of God is sincere. While traveling from the place where we cling always to our will to the place where we always do God's will, we sometimes wonder if we have lost the way. We know that we advance his kingdom by prayer and love, but sometimes we wonder whether we should go on delivering mail, or join the Peace Corps instead? Pursue a career in advertising, or work for a Christian publication? Take a part-time job, or spend our free hours volunteering to read to nursing-home patients?

Usually we are right where God wants us. Whatever task he has put into our hands, whether it is collecting garbage or running a country, whatever people he has put in our lives, whether they are cantankerous do-nothings or ambitious celebrities, form the setting of our relationship with him. If we feel called to make a change, we submit it to prayer and then make the best decision we can. If we are fortunate enough to have a spiritual director, he or she can help us discern the action of God. If by chance we make a wrong decision in good faith and God wants us elsewhere, he will see to it we get there. If ordinary means fail, God has any number of alternate methods at his disposal.

Saul had been sent by his father to find some lost donkeys when Samuel, the prophet, told him God had chosen him to become king of Israel (1 Samuel 9:3–10:1). Joan of Arc was told by the archangel Michael to leave her mother's house and lead an army. The prophet Habakkuk was taking stew to harvesters in the fields when an angel told him to take the food to Babylon and give it to Daniel, who was in the lions' den (Daniel 14:33–39).

Apparently Habakkuk thought there was some mistake. "Babylon, sir, I have never seen," he protested, "and I do not know the den!" Whereupon the angel carried him off by his hair and set him at the edge of the den. Certainly God had other means of feeding Daniel. He might have made a meal appear miraculously before him. He could have sent ravens with food in their beaks or done a number of other things, but it pleased him to use Habakkuk.

We don't need to waste energy fretting about whether we are where God wants us to be. If we make mistakes in discerning his will for us, he has ways to correct them.

The angel transported Habakkuk back to his own country, where presumably he resumed his interrupted task of taking food to the field workers. But what of Daniel, so unexpectedly provided with room service? He didn't seem in the least amazed. What is a meal provided by such means from the God who is Lord of all?

"You have remembered me, O God," Daniel said calmly, "you have not forsaken those who love you" (Daniel 14:38). And rising to his feet, he ate the meal.

Daniel's equanimity was the fruit of complete confidence in God. As a boy, he had been chosen from among the captive Israelites to be trained for service at the court of the Babylonian king. He and other young captives were to be fed from the king's table on meat and wine. This would mean breaking the dietary prohibitions of the Mosaic law. Rather than do so, Daniel asked to be served only vegetables and water (Daniel 1:3–16).

His request could well have meant death. Obviously Daniel was ready to die, even as a youth, rather than turn aside from the path of God. For most of us, such trust comes slowly. God leads us to trust him first in smaller things.

We become aware that our trust is very limited and resides in ourselves. We buy groceries to last as many days as our storage space will hold, clothes for several seasons in advance. We make investments for financial returns years in the future. We have learned the lesson of the grasshopper and the ant only too well. All this we list as need.

In this world there are many who live in true need, with one ragged garment for all seasons, with little shelter or none, without food for more than one meal in several days. How often are we nudged to help

68

support a child in the Third World, for instance, only to find ourselves shaking our heads because we haven't the means? We have two children in college at the same time and a third coming along. Our parents have retired and need some help making ends meet. There are medical bills, housing expenses. Every cent has been wrung out of the budget. It is just not possible to help the less fortunate.

But of course it is. What stops us is not lack of means, but lack of trust. God never asks us to take the food out of our children's mouths, but he does ask us to share what we have. As we grow spiritually, our trust in him grows. We realize he knows our situation; he will not let generosity go unnoticed.

"If anyone wants to go to law over your shirt, give him your coat as well," Christ says (Matthew 5:40). That sounds like the height of madness. But consider: if you saw one of your children generously sharing with a sibling, wouldn't you be touched by it? Wouldn't you feel so pleased and so moved by love for that generous child that you would see to it she didn't suffer for her generosity, and maybe even reward her as well?

God likes to see us share. It shows him we love others out of the overflow of our love for him and his for us. It is a concrete gesture of trust in him. And if we all lived as he taught us, we would know that anyone who gave a coat away would soon be given a replacement by someone similarly prompted to share.

We don't share easily. We cling to our belongings, using them as an indication of status and cleverness. Who of us hasn't "needed" a new car when the old one shows signs of wear? Who doesn't "need" a new outfit for a special occasion? We "need" dairy products and eggs and fish, meat and fruit and grain; and then we have to diet to lose excess weight. We "need" our cigarettes and our vacation time, our trips away and our nights out.

Sharing is not easy. Giving part of what we want to keep for ourselves is almost as hard as losing an arm. Yet sharing is one of the things God brings us to, and when we find ourselves truly concerned for his needy, giving to them as an act of love and trust, we know God has worked an unseen miracle. He has softened our hearts, brought light and spaciousness to the neglected mansion where he dwells within us, and leads us to complete and absolute trust in him.

CHRIST AND POSSESSIONS

As the body's demands are disciplined, we grow more aware of our spirit. The attempts of the world to deny and stifle our spiritual life become more obvious to us. Those endless ads for shampoo and mouthwash, clothes and vitamins—where are the ads asking, "Have you fed your soul today? Have you had your soul cleaned recently? If you should die suddenly, how are you fixed for soul insurance?" Even with people who hunger for God, the world succeeds too well in dismissing the spirit. We find ourselves engaged in a battle with ourselves and with the world, but prayer deepens our faith, and in its light we see the things of God more clearly.

God, tutoring us in his ways, makes us aware of the divergence between what we need and what the world tells us we need. If we are listening, we develop an aversion to excess. In general our needs are little but our greed is great. We don't even realize how greedy we are, for the process of freeing us from the burden of many things is generally a long one, and at the beginning we sometimes feel we are being overly deprived. But think: do we really need a pair of purple shoes because purple is the in-color this season? Do we need a five-course lunch and a seven-course dinner? A television set in the bedroom, the kitchen, and the den? Four watches? Three complete sets of dishes? Throw rugs over the orientals over the wall-to-wall broadloom? The list is endless.

As our prayer grows and deepens, we realize we need only God, for when we have him all else is given to us. Jesus taught us to pray for our daily bread (Matthew 6:11, Luke 11:3) and told us not to be anxious about physical necessities, because, "Your heavenly Father knows all that you need. Seek first his kingship over you . . . and all these things will be given you besides" (Matthew 6:33).

Little by little, we surrender the things that hold us back from loving God more fully. As we are less influenced by advertising or the need to match our neighbor's possessions with better ones, we become more free. When the teachings of Christ start to bear fruit in our lives, we see how great is the darkness in which we have lived. The goods of the world that once so captured our hearts become nothing, less than nothing. As our greed dies, we find with some astonishment that our needs are few and simple and don't require twenty-hour workdays chasing after money to provide them. The rat race ceases to exist. In its place we enjoy tranquility. Life takes on a less hectic pace. Tension eases as we realize that God, and not the world, provides our sustenance. Our lives are stripped of unnecessary clutter.

When you come down to it, God has a strange outlook on financial security. "You fool!" Christ called the man who planned on building granaries to hold his surplus harvest. "This very night your life shall be required of you" (Luke 12:20). He instructed his hearers to "stop worrying, then, over questions like, 'What are we to eat, or what are we to drink, or what are we to wear?' The unbelievers are always running after these things" (Matthew 6:31, 32). His followers were to seek the kingdom of God and trust in their heavenly Father, not in themselves. "Give us each day our daily bread," Jesus taught us to pray (Matthew 6:11, Luke 11:3). He didn't suggest we ask for goods for a year, or a decade, or a lifetime. God seems to like having us live in his hand, acknowledging him as the Giver of all things. He wants our spirits to be serene and confident in the knowledge that he will care for us, and not burden ourselves and dissipate our energy worrying over material acquisitions.

This is not to suggest that he will support us in idleness. We are to work. But when we take care to seek him first, he takes care of us. Sometimes he chooses that we should be givers, sharing what he has given us. At other times we must be takers, accepting what he prompts others to give. When giving, we are exercised in charity; when receiving, in humility.

When St. Teresa of Jesus made plans to found her convent of St. Joseph and learned absolutely no money was available for the undertaking, she exclaimed, "Good! Now I know it is of the Lord."

When the Curé of Ars was told there was no corn left to feed the orphans he was caring for, he went to the empty loft and prayed. When mealtime came, the loft was filled with corn.

When St. Frances of Rome was forbidden by her father-in-law to distribute any more of the family's goods to the hungry during a famine, she too prayed. God filled an empty warehouse with grain so she could continue her charity.

In that case, says the skeptic, why doesn't he feed the Third World?

During our earthly lives, God works ordinarily through us. Have you ever felt prompted to donate to these suffering people and quashed the impulse? If everyone so prompted listened and obeyed, we might have some justification for challenging God on the issue. If we gave what we could, and also prayed, the results might astonish us.

CONCERN FOR OTHERS

As we grow in love of God, we see more clearly the sufferings of our brothers and sisters. Love prompts us to act. In addition to praying for people, we find ourselves sharing our goods with them. God takes us further, and we share our time. Some of us open our homes to parentless children or solitary old folks in need of shelter. Others are active in hospitals, nursing homes, schools, and children's residences. Some of us may be drawn to battle for social justice, for civil rights, for an end to violence.

Love is not passive. We cannot love God without loving others, and love means extending ourselves in whatever way we are called to be living examples of the love and the constant providence of God for others.

FIVE

Getting Answers to Your Prayers

Does God answer prayers? Your prayers?
Anyone's prayers? The miracles of Christ
and the lives of the saints give many
examples that show he does, but we've
always harbored a suspicion that God plays
favorites, listening when his saints speak
but turning a deaf ear to ordinary folks.
Filling rooms with grain, as he did for the
Curé of Ars and St. Frances of Rome,
strikes us as something of a grandstand
play. Why doesn't he give us the car or
house or job we ask him for? If God
actually answered prayers more often, he
might have more of a following! What is
the point of praying about things when as

far as we can see absolutely nothing happens? *Does* God answer prayers?

He answers a number of mine, although for many years my requests seemed to fall into a vacuum despite his promise that, "Whatever you ask for in my name I will do, so as to glorify the Father in the Son" (John 14:13). Can God lie? Did the evangelist forget to take down a few qualifying clauses, such as, "Whatever you ask for in my name I will do, if it won't harm you in any way, and if it will bring you closer to God, and if you submit your request in the proper form, and if I feel like granting requests that day? I always felt that asking God for anything was similar to buying a sweepstakes ticket. Maybe your entry would be the one chosen from among millions. If you didn't hit the jackpot, you could try again when your luck might be better.

I can't say God never answered my prayers. Like every child, there were school days when I prayed for the bell to ring, and it rang; for snow to fall in the night, and it fell; for a test I wasn't ready for to be postponed, and it was. But he never came through when I wanted magic, like being able to fly, or when I wanted to get out of a chore: "I'll go out and play, God, and you send some angels to clean my room while I'm gone." Alas, the angels were occupied elsewhere.

As I grew older I decided any childhood requests that had been "answered" were only coincidences, and I stopped asking for such silly things. Then with adulthood came the conviction that God only hears prayers for spiritual things. You pray in a lackluster kind of way for a better job or for an illness to be healed, not expecting to be heard for years, if ever. And if you don't get the job or the illness drags on, you shrug and say, "God knows best."

But what about his promise "Whatever you ask . . .?" That must be one of the passages to be taken symbolically, not literally. Forget it.

GOD ALWAYS LISTENS

It was with great astonishment that I realized God had always been listening. He began saying yes about ten years ago. At that point I was in midlife, barely past the initial surrender. Yet God made me aware he was calling me to an even deeper intimacy with him, and part of that call seemed to involve exploring contemplative life.

One July day I found myself in the garden of a local convent. Although determined to follow wherever God might lead, I was full of apprehension. Would the heavy front door clang shut behind me forever? This religious order was one of prayer and penance. I could learn the prayer part, but penance? The word had a medieval and forbidding sound. I was an artist, a musician and writer, used to dramatic expression of every trifling emotion, addicted to parties and good fellowship, a slave to comfort.

I hope this is God, I thought to myself. Otherwise it is sheer insanity.

However lenient "penance" has become in these post-Vatican II days, I knew that in this convent it would still embrace fasting in some form, and I was a compulsive eater. Anyone with the problem will understand that even the idea of fasting is enough to chill the blood. An eater severed from her favorite foods is like an addict without drugs, an alcoholic with nothing but water to drink. But if this was what God wanted, he would make it possible.

Sure he would. Wouldn't he?

During the course of our conversation, Mother Superior, who seemed to intuitively understand what a weakling she had before her, left to bring us something to drink. I determined to accept whatever it was, but I reminded the Lord how much I disliked tea and coffee. How I would like a tall glass of lemonade!

Sister returned with lemonade. A small coincidence.

I am allergic to fish, but was determined to dine on it if that was the custom of the house.

Roast turkey appeared. Was God playing games? It was almost as though he had said, "I am aware of you, my timid, fearful creature. I know your needs and your fears. Trust me."

I began to hope. Sugar is my addiction, and it hadn't escaped my notice that the sisters ate sparingly, using food as fuel and not as an unbridled pleasure. Sweets, Lord! Surely if I become one of these holy nuns, I'll never see sweets again.

My visit coincided with the feast of the patron saint of the order, and a number of guest confections had been donated for the occasion. "Silly child," God seemed to say, "Do you prove me with candy and muffins, when all that is, is mine to give?"

By now these coincidences seemed too coincidental to be innocent. Okay, God. Here's a toughie. How about clams? Better yet, lobster?

Both appeared shortly before dinnertime, donated at the door. Both were enough of a rarity that the sisters were not sure how to prepare them. Lobster has not made an appearance there since.

God was meeting me where I was, reassuring me in that rather comical way that he knew me completely, loved me absolutely, and would take care of my most childish needs. He has since led me to a place of such trust in him that, yes, if I prayed to him to remove a mountain, I would expect it to go. Because nothing is difficult for God. The hardest thing he does we hardly notice; he softens our hearts, toward him and one another.

STEPS TO HAVING PRAYERS ANSWERED

Discipleship

"I chose you to go forth and bear fruit . . . so that all you ask of the Father in my name he will give you" (John 15:16).

When Christ promised anything that was asked, he was speaking to his disciples. And he made it plain that his disciples had to give more than lip-service. "None of those who cry out, 'Lord, Lord,' will enter the kingdom of God, but only the one who does the will of my Father in heaven" (Matthew 7:21).

Those who keep Christ's commandments acknowledge him to the depths of their being as God, the Creator, the One. They surrender to his will, a lifelong process during which they discern more and more clearly how God is leading them, and grow more sensitive and prompt in their response. The initial surrender seems to be the turning point in moving from being a follower to being a true disciple.

From that point we yield more fully to the King of Love. Love becomes the touchstone of our lives. Love informs and sustains our lives, and we cleanse ourselves of all that is not love.

As we grow more sensitive to God and increase in our love, the power of sin—which is simply no-love, the absolute contrary of love—has less influence over us. As two opposites cannot exist to their fullest degree in one organism, love drives out no-love and the whole train of evil effects that accompany it. In loving, we become more like God and take on the family resemblance of goodness and love.

St. John of the Cross tells us that the soul completely surrendered to God has all its motions guided by him. There is nothing in that soul contrary to the will of God, nothing to impede his action or turn his grace aside. The soul wills what God wills, and desires nothing that God does not desire.

To reach so great a degree of union of will with God is the work of a lifetime and very few attain it. Like a married couple well-suited to each other who seem to read each other's minds and anticipate each other's desires, the person and God correspond.

They are attuned to each other's likes and tastes, and know how best to delight each other.

This great unity of will with God is the prime reason why great saints received such spectacular answers to their prayers. For them, "Whatever you ask," is literally true. Being so closely attuned to God's will, they never desire anything contrary to his wishes in any situation. Their prayers are answered.

Since few of us will ever reach such heights of sanctity, God fortunately hears us and loves us wherever we are on the road. After our initial surrender of will, he seems to act more openly in our lives. If you have reached this point, you know for yourself that your prayers are answered with greater frequency. If you have not yet reached it, pray for the grace to do so. That prayer will certainly be answered!

Confidence

"Ask in faith, never doubting, for the doubter is like the surf tossed and driven by the wind. A man of this sort, devious and erratic in all that he does, must not expect to receive anything from the Lord" (James 1:7,8).

Everyone knows the old story about the congregation assembled to pray for rain, and not a single member brought an umbrella. When we ask for things in prayer, in the depth of our heart we are convinced either that God will not listen or will not act. Yet we should come to him for help with the same innocent, complete confidence your child has when he shows you a splinter in his finger. He knows you will take care of it. He has no doubt at all.

Of course some prayers haven't much chance because we are asking God to act in ways totally alien to him. "God, please make me rich," is not likely to find favor. Neither is, "Please let me win the million-dollar-plus lottery."

If you want to be rich, you'll get there faster by working for it than by asking it of God. Jesus warned us that riches are an obstacle to entering the kingdom of heaven. When we are buttressed by wealth, we lose our sense of dependency and risk straying from him. He is not going to help us do that, nor will he respond to our greed.

But if you or your family need anything for this day, go to him and tell him what is lacking. Do you need a place to live? Money for medical bills? Food for this day? Hold out your hand in perfect confidence that he will fill it. He will.

To pray, "Lord, make me thin," "Lord, make me beautiful," "Lord, make me ambitious," is not likely to get a positive response either. When we ask God to "make" us anything, we are in effect asking him to take over part of our will and program it outside of our control. God wants us to develop our own strengths.

To pray, "Lord, help me overcome my compulsive eating," or drinking, or gambling, gets results. One prayer is the creature acting. The other is the creature being acted upon. God created us for freedom, not slavery.

The saints made some strange requests in complete confidence, and they were answered. St. Teresa of Jesus, holding an infant relative, prayed that if the child were not to grow up to know and love God, but would lose his soul, God should take the child then and there. God did, much to the mother's anger and dismay.

Anna Catherine Emmerich was late joining her mother for Mass one Sunday because she couldn't find her neckerchief. She was afraid her mother would note the lack and scold her. She prayed, and felt a kerchief being placed about her neck as she ran to catch up with the family. When Anna Catherine had a chance to look at the neckerchief she had a new worry. It was so much finer than her own, she was sure her mother would ask her questions about it that she wouldn't be able to answer.

We don't have to be great saints for God to be aware of our needs and hear us. Once in church I was complaining to God at great length. He seemed to be crushing me with a series of physical setbacks; a heart constantly out of rhythm, chronic bronchitis, diabetes. And the final blow: five teeth needing root canals.

Just whose side are you on, God?

In the silence, I had a sense of being reassured. Did I want a small proof of his constant love? Choose. He would do whatever I desired.

I felt able to cope with the illnesses, but those teeth were the final straw. The dentist had already done a root canal on one side, hoping it would take care of both teeth there; but that still left three on the other side.

God plays love-games with us. To bear with abscessed teeth certainly isn't much in comparison with the suffering he bore for us, but it was too much for me. It seemed almost as if he smiled, a loving Father just out of sight, bemused as a father is touched by the actions of his small children who are not aware he is silently watching.

On my next visit the dentist took a new set of x-rays to determine what treatment to follow. We had both seen x-rays of these teeth before and knew what to expect. But God had put his finger in.

"Look." The dentist pointed to the first x-ray. "This tooth has what we call a natural root canal. It is as if a dentist had done the work. Here, you can see the canal on the film."

There it was before my eyes.

"The next two teeth that were abscessed show no signs of abscess." He indicated the root area, which in previous x-rays had been nothing but a black hole. "The entire membrane of the tooth is visible. The roots have no shadow.

"It happens sometimes." the dentist said. "We don't know why."

I know why. Prayer power.

Thanksgiving

When God does us a favor, he likes to be thanked. How often would you do favors for somebody who never acknowledged them? Remember Jesus' question to the one leper of the ten who returned to thank him for his healing: "Where are the other nine?" (Luke 17:17).

God is constantly doing things for us of which we are unaware. The least we can do is thank him for the favors we are conscious of. Aside from the courtesy involved, which is no more than we would extend to another person like ourselves, we should be mindful that we owe all we are and have to God, who keeps us in his loving care even when we ignore him.

So there you have it, a primer for getting prayers answered: (1) *discipleship*, which means acknowledging God as Lord of all that is and doing our best to follow the way Christ taught us, including yielding our will to his in all things; (2) *confidence*, as a result of this yielding becoming more and more alert to God's ways, more attuned to his will, asking favors in complete confidence of his ability and desire to grant them; and (3) *thanksgiving*, having received everything from his hand, we are careful to thank him.

WHEN GOD DOESN'T SEEM TO LISTEN

Sometimes God seems to say no. Keep praying. The Israelites cried out to God for four hundred years before he led them out of Egypt.

Often, because we are new to God's ways, we desire something that is not in our best interests. Sometimes we beg for a physical healing when it would be more in accord with God's will to ask for patience and endurance. If after much praying he seems to be ignoring our request, we might ask him to guide us in knowing what his will is in the situation.

As we grow closer to him, God teaches us to see beneath the appearances of things to the truth of what he is doing or has done. A situation that on the surface seems wrong may be very right. The crucifixion is a telling example. The forces of hell must have gloated with victory—Satan had seemed to overcome God. Yet we know that moment of seemingly greatest triumph for evil was the moment of its greatest defeat. The death of Christ destroyed evil. His death was not defeat, but supreme glory.

On the surface, sickness is always evil. We know it cannot be good, or there would be sickness in heaven. Instead of alleviating illness, Christ would have been dispensing it. One day it will exist no more. Until then, sickness and suffering are evils none of us escape. When Christ redeemed us, his death broke the back of the evil that had gripped the world since the fall, but it is as if the monster, in its death throes, still has its jaws firmly clamped on the world. There is a space between the vanquishing of evil and the release of that death grip. With every day that passes, the grip lessens.

Meantime, although we know that such suffering, endured patiently, helps strengthen us supernaturally, we should have no qualms about asking Christ to relieve it. Christ wants us whole and happy. That is what resurrection is all about. If he permits us to suffer, we can trust that it is leading us to wholeness, just as his suffering led to restoring the wholeness of the entire human race. If he relieves our suffering, we thank him.

SIX

The Challenge of Praying

As God leads us more deeply into his love, we find ourselves being transformed. We become increasingly aware of others and able to love them. We are more patient and compassionate, relieved of the necessity of proving to all comers how wonderful we are and how insignificant they are. We live in great interior joy and freedom that nothing seems able to change, and from hour to hour we are more in love with our God.

God, who was a stranger, a pious myth, has become our friend and lover, the companion of our lives. He is the central reality, the unfailing comforter, the yardstick by which everything else is measured. Where once we hardly thought of him, now we refer everything to him.

Our lives become ordered according to everlasting priorities, with the paradoxical result of making us more effective in our daily tasks. We seem to be anchored firmly in life, able to withstand the severest storms with equanimity. Although hardships don't cease and the way is often dark and difficult, the love of Christ illumines all and draws us always deeper into his heart.

We find great pleasure in spiritual reading and are eager to learn all we can from the lives of the saints, who have traveled the road before us. Scripture becomes a never-ending source of wonder. Now when we curl up with a Good Book, it is the best!

We are eager to show our ever-increasing love by whatever way God gives us, and we rejoice when he allows us to work more directly for him or for the advance of his kingdom. Yes, we are changed indeed.

As God draws us nearer to him, he increases our appreciation of Our Lady. Some people feel that to honor Mary takes away a degree of glory from Christ, that we should pray to God and God alone. Of course God is unique, transcendent, the One, and Mary is a creature like ourselves.

Yet she has her unique mission in the Church. Christ gave her to us as mother. How ungrateful of us to turn from so generous a gift.

Purists insist that Christ alone is the Way. True. But Mary is the lamp that lights the way. She leads us and encourages us in our journey. She adds her petitions to ours, enhancing our prayer and flavoring it with her love.

Devotion to Mary, far from detracting from the honor we give to God, adds to it, for when we say, "Mary," she in turn says, "Lord." Her heart is entirely his and was from the beginning, and her greatest desire is to bring all souls to him. Love her and let her love you. Beseech her to teach you to love her Son as she does, fully and forever.

The office of the Blessed Virgin Mary calls Mary mother and daughter of the King of Kings, the seat from whom arose the Sun of Justice, Christ, our Lord. She was the tabernacle of the infant Church. Venerate her highly and hold her dear.

The saints and angels, too, can help us. Loving God entirely, they love all who love him. Besotted lovers, as we ourselves shall be one day, they overflow with love of him and delight in helping increase the love of others for him. Having gone the painful way of earth that we ourselves are traveling, they have an acute sympathy for our difficulties and are there to befriend and aid us.

God leads each soul exquisitely in a dance composed for it alone. There are as many ways of praying as there are those who pray. In prayer, let him lead you as he wishes, from silence to speech, from vocal prayer to quiet. In his time, he will lead you to contemplation. He works on us like a sculptor on soft clay, molding us, rounding the sharp corners, softening the lines. All he asks of us is not to resist him but to be docile under his touch, knowing it is the touch of perfect love.

Now we are on the road to praying always, as he told us to do, for prayer is the expression of our love for God. We grow more and more aware of his invisible presence, for love makes us aware, just as we would be conscious of a human lover. His presence is a constant, a given; not in a way that disrupts the work he has given us to do in the world, but in a way that enhances it and gives it meaning. To pray always is simply to be always loving God. To be holy is simply to live in his will at every moment.

Jesus told us what it is to pray and to live the Christian life.

"You are the salt of the earth. . . . You are

the light of the world. . . . Your light must shine before men so that they may see goodness in your acts and give praise to your heavenly Father" (Matthew 5:13, 14, 16).

"Offer no resistance to injury. . . . Give to the man who begs from you. Do not turn your back on the borrower. . . . Love your enemies, pray for your persecutors. This will prove that you are sons of your heavenly Father" (Matthew 5:39,42,44,45).

"When you are praying, do not behave like the hypocrites who love to stand and pray in synagogues or on street corners in order to be noticed. I give you my word, they are already repaid. Whenever you pray, go to your room, close the door, and pray to your Father in private. Then your Father, who sees what no man sees, will repay you" (Matthew 6:5,6).

"If you forgive the faults of others, your heavenly Father will forgive you yours. If you do not forgive others, neither will your Father forgive you" (Matthew 6:14,15).

"Do not lay up for yourselves an earthly treasure. Moths and rust corrode; thieves break in and steal. . . . Remember, where your treasure is, there your heart is also" (Matthew 6:19,21).

"Seek first his kingship over you, his way of holiness, and all these things will be given you besides. Enough, then, of worrying about tomorrow. Let tomorrow take care of itself. Today has troubles enough of its own" (Matthew 6:33,34).

"If you want to avoid judgment, stop passing judgment. Your verdict on others will be the verdict passed on you. The measure with which you measure will be used to measure you" (Matthew 7:1,2).

"Ask, and you will receive. Seek, and you will find. Knock, and it will be opened to you. For the one who asks, receives. The one who seeks, finds. The one who knocks, enters" (Matthew 7:7,8).

"Would one of you hand his son a stone when he asks for a loaf, or a poisonous snake when he asks for a fish? If you, with all your sins, know how to give your children what is good, how much more will your heavenly Father give good things to anyone who asks him!" (Matthew 7:9–11).

Do you dare accept Christ's challenge? Are you willing to walk more closely with him, knowing it will change your priorities and attitudes and give you a different outlook on everything in this life? Do you want to draw closer to him now, knowing that he is the reason for which we were created and the purpose of our life, now and in eternity?

The following prayer, author unknown, seems to say it all.

Father,

The most profound thing you have given to me is the knowledge that Jesus is Lord. It is easy for me to *say* that "Jesus is Lord." It is wonderful, joyful, comforting. But to let Jesus *be* Lord is quite another thing. It is far easier said than done.

It means to stop living my life and instead to lead his life. This means not doing anything for myself anymore, but only for others; nothing for myself, only for him. Sacrifice isn't adequate. Dying is what is called for. This dying will take time, but I ask his help and begin. Knowing the cost full well, I pray—

Dear Jesus,

Be my Lord. Help me to die that you might live. Help me to give you all those things in my life that are now more important to me than you are; all those things that obscure you.

Take my pride, my selfishness, my self-centeredness, my lust for earthly things, my angers, my hostilities. Then, Lord Jesus, take my resentments and frustrations, my despair. Finally, Lord, take my will and make it yours. Cleanse me and purify me, Lord.

Enable me to empty myself of myself that I may be a worthy dwelling place for you and for the Father. Enable me to become centered on you alone; to be opened, sensitive, receptive, and attuned to the guidance of your Spirit.

And then truly become my Lord, Jesus. Manifest yourself in my life. Make my life that real witness to you; a mystery so great that it is explained only by your existence.

Let my life become one that does for others what you would do. A life that begins to give back in some small way all you have given to me.

Thank you, Jesus. May you be praised forever.

Amen.